Charles A. Compton

Consistency of the Normal Metes and Bounds of our Republic

A Jewel From Which the People Should be Loathe to Part

Charles A. Compton

Consistency of the Normal Metes and Bounds of our Republic
A Jewel From Which the People Should be Loathe to Part

ISBN/EAN: 9783337007812

Printed in Europe, USA, Canada, Australia, Japan

Cover: Foto ©Suzi / pixelio.de

More available books at **www.hansebooks.com**

CONSISTENCY

OF THE NORMAL METES AND BOUNDS

Of Our Republic.

A JEWEL

From Which the People Should be Loathe to Part.

SPIRIT OF JEFFERSON PRINT, CHARLES TOWN, W. VA.

"Think well. One good thought,
Known to be thine own,
Is better than a thousand gleaned
From fields by others sown."

SELECTED.

I write not for the sake of party, merely. God forbid that I should. I write for the sake of principle. However, if the party adapts itself to the principle, then I am found of the party.

"Volitions make acts; acts oft repeated form habits; habits long continued build character; character shapes destiny; and not even the Creator himself ever changes destiny." What is our nation's will?

PREFACE.

My Dear Observer.—In the name of God and for the sake of humanity, I ask you to likewise consider this little work from beginning to end, and give it the public endorsement which it deserves. It may have weaknesses, but it is laden with truth.

I am only a man of ordinary circumstances, teaching a primary school in the woods, on a hillside, in the Eastern Panhandle of the "Little Mountain State" of West Virginia, but I am happily contented with my present attainments in life and an humble submission of my future to fate. I am as well contented as the President in his chair can be, and above other things I owe this to my religious inclinations, my ability of judgment, and the quality of my predominant volitions; whatever they may be considered by others to be.

"The rust shall find the sword of fame,
The dust shall hide the crown,
No man shall nail so high his name,
Time will not tear it down."

"The happiest heart that ever beat,
Was in some quiet breast
That breathed the common daylight sweet,
And left to heaven the rest."

For this work, I must say that I am strongly inclined to regard it as an inspiration wrought through a chain of Divine mysteries, and penetrating the veil which separates the human within from the superhuman without, to our people.

I am now confident that in less than one month, by applying my spare moments while teaching school, I have written a work that will be sold by its millions, and read by people of many nations. It will be thought of in field, shop and home. It will be quoted from the pulpit and impersonated on the stage. It will gradually gain admittance to the hearts of a vast people, and be found woven, here and there, in the warp and woof of the garment that shall clothe the weal of all good governments.

"Truth, crushed to earth, shall rise again,
The eternal years of God are hers;
While error, wounded, writhes in pain
And dies among her worshipers."

CHAPTER I.

This little work will give a partial vent to the fiery feelings which have been kindling within me for some time past. The friction, caused by the poiicical cunning and treachery of the times, coming in contact with my regard for our beloved country, has created within my soul an ardent heat, which can only be abated by the soothing cognizance that the principles and doctrines which I so much cherish, and deem essential to the prosperity and longevity of our free institutions have culminated in law, proven worthy in fair probation, and found a safe lodgment in the hearts of the American People.

I have never taken any very active part in politics farther than to remonstrate or approve in a conversational way when opportunities were presented. I have had no motives in view more than to ground deeper and deeper in the public mind those cardinai principles upon which the very foundation of our republic rests. I am stemming the current of existence by the aid of no political ring or clique, and far less do I help to control any; on the other hand, as is the case with many an innocent voter today, there are local organizations rife about me which have certainly been trying to tempt my stability, by holding out allurements to lead me away from high ideals and virtuous Democratic principles. But in battling the giants with the weapon of patriotism, thanks to Protecting Omnipotence, I have become stronger, and am very proud of the fact that I have an unfettered and unrestricted right of suffrage which none can dispute; an independent vote, the complement of a free will, which is in full accord with the principles of democracy, and in complete abhorrance with aristocracies and monarchies, especially when they are found lurking deceitfully under the cloak of Republicanism and charging stealthily against our freedom.

My anxiety is very much alert over other great victories, which our people must win or suffer ignominy in defeat, such as the *Downfall of Trusts*, the *Overthrow of High Tariff*, the mother of trusts, and the *Peaceable Restoration of Silver;* but, in my humble and unselfish opinion, a greater victory than any of these lies in the *Solution of the Entanglements* into which our recent war with Spain has placed us, in such a manner as to rebuke once and for all time, any idea of adopting a policy of domineering colonial expansion and to be very wary of any other.

If these questions are not settled in opposition to a colonial policy, any sensible person, by taking a glance at the pages of history and the present geographical and social conditions of the civilized world, will agree that our great republic, which we proudly call "The Colossus of The Americas," has reached the zenith of its glory, and that sooner or later will be heard such expressions as "Westward the course of empire takes its way," with the true literal ring to them, and amid lamentations instead of hurrahs.

I believe the defeat of the colonial expansion policy is just at this time paramount to all other issues, because the other issues have to deal with conditions which have assumed such braggart proportions and such arrogancy in their approach that they cannot repulse the requisite attention and vigilance of our people; because so direct in their effects, we may hope to see their speedy settlement without curtailing the life of the republic. We are now a strong people, materially and intellectually, and the giant of dangerous conditions with which other issues have to deal shall not have *deceitfully* gained strength too vast for us to control, before exciting and creating within us indignation and righteous contempt sufficient to result in his downfall. But the modern giant of the abnormal expansion of our American Republic, though yet in his incipiency, causes me to shudder with fear for the safety of our one cherished hope—that the long life of our nation, as a republic, may surpass that of all the other nations of the earth, demonstrating to the world that just governments do derive their powers from the consent of the governed.

This colonial expansion policy, especially if it is successful at first, appears to my mind as a great sneaking, lurking, chronic disorder of the nation,. which is certain of direful consequences. As great reforms are not wrought instantly, even more so, the gradual shifting from one condition to another which leads to the corruption, decay and downfall of nations is usually slow in its progress; and to be sensible to it, it seems that the human mind has to somewhat magnify its conceptions. And yet, not so, as with reforms, this "shifting" towards decay of nations is likely to begin at any time when the people are not vigilant. Broad and deep must be our minds, and grand and noble and unselfish our purposes would we comprehend what it is, and steer the old Ship of State clear of it. It is so slow in its progress that could one notice the growing of the feathers on a duck he might not observe this shifting.

So, why not pardon the McKinley administration for allowing it to begin this shifting by adopting a colonial government, his "taxation without tryanny" in the Philippines? But there are things we can perceive with the eye and understand with the ear, and there are things we can be conscious of; therefore, as we have reason to believe that the McKinley administration, in trying to rule conscious beings should have conscious men at its helm, we must place the responsibility where it belongs. Shall we graft this bud of a colonial policy upon our national institutions? If so, it shall certainly grow, blossom sometime, and sooner or later ripen into its ultimate fruit—the ruins of the republic. The bud which puts forth the blossom is wonderfully, yet attentively nurtured by mother nature, and the blossom develops into fruit which sometimes ripens in early summer, sometimes in late October. Ah! what future generation is it that, by our vote and voice, we shall cause to utter the lamentable wail, "Had we not had the bud we should not have the fruit!"

A certain class of politicians may preach that a colonial policy on such a small scale can not hurt us, and that it will bring vast revenues into our treasury, and the like; but, my friends, I exhort you, with all candor, that you be not misled. To adopt their colonizing schemes, would be setting a dangerous example, which may or may not be followed for a generation, an example lurking and direful in its consequences, an example which would be referred to as a precedent in making future decisions.

If we should adopt a colonial policy, the better we should get along with our colonies, the worse it would ultimately be for us, and the worse we should get along with them the better it would ultimately be for us. A burnt child dreads the fire, if he is not burnt up in it, and will learn to keep away from it, but if he continues to play about it without receiving little burns, he is liable at some time in the future to be consumed in one great conflagration. The McKinley administration might get children to play with colonial fire, but they will surely have a task to get Uncle Sam into it.

Suppose we should recognize the giant of expansion and adopt a colonial policy and get it in charming good working order. Greed is never satisfied. The shifting changes of time would, sooner or later, make it possible for us to fasten our grip upon something more, and we could not withstand the temptation. We would say look at the glorious colonial policy of President McKinley. And we might continue various forms of expansion, when slightest opportunities were presented, and reach out farther and farther until we had absorbed the whole American Continent and the islands of the sea. All this might be accomplished in a few decades, and again, it may require centuries. Who can tell by looking at the blossom whether the apple shall ripen in June or October? And yet who would not agree that it is a sign of fruit? Patriots of America, have you brains? I am loathe to believe otherwise than that you have, and of a superior quality, too. Then use them in exercising a little practical love for your country.

Imagine we should reach the collossal development I have just described. What glory gould there be in it. For then, and long before that time, would we see corruption, which would be sustained by low designing statesmen, and sectional jealously, as a natural consequence of various social, climatic and geographical differences, gnawing at our very vitals and calling down the doom of empires old. Our great Civil War was chiefly the result of natural sectional differences, as everybody will agree; and if it was a result of natural sectional differances in our home country, who can imagine the extent of the liabilities we would incur, by extending our national wings, and brooding over all races, and all the various sectional differences and conditions from the North Pole to the South Pole, through all the zones and amid all climes? The Civil war was more of an acute disease than this colonial expansion malady is likely to be. We could tell better what remedies to apply to it, and how. We could better endure a dozen such civil strifes at different intervals than be plagued with this chronic expansion trouble. The best thing to do with it is to "nip it in the bud," before it gets to spreading, or it will attack all the vital organs of Uncle Sam's being, and then no remedy, save death only, can relieve the grand old victim.

If we should assume the proportions to which I have alluded, then and perhaps while insatiate greed is planning for the possession of Australia for a potato patch, great civil strifes are liable to loom up and result in the nation's downfall. How easy it would be for the Southern States to join the outh American Republics and remove our capital, our modern Rome, to a modern Constantinople; and what facilities there would be for the Northern States to join Canada and do the same thing. Shall we drift into policies to achieve all this vain glory, or shall we rather adhere to the patriotism of our forefathers, and preserve the nation, which they conceived for us, in sacred trust? I am opposed to expansion! and I would say it loudly!

I believe it was never intended that one nation should rule the earth; and history corroborates the assertion. Nations, as well as human beings, were intended to have a normal size and a social spirit, and the greater the departure from these natural conditions, the greater will be dame nature's punishment, for she is impartial. (But we should remember, though, that nations are, naturally, only convenient dummies which have people to do their thinking for them.) Methinks, the normal size and the social spirit of nations is a sublime thought. What man of 150 pounds of usefulness is it that would desire to take on 75 pounds more of corpulency and corruption, thus jeopordizing his health and pleasure? So we should think for our Grand Dummy. I believe the normal metes and bounds of our country are fairly established; and I mean without Hawaii, without Cuba, without Porto Rico, without the Philippines. Upon the map of the world our country presents an appearance of neatness and location, and a location of which I am proud. I give my hand and my heart to the cause of anti-expansion, and in the language of Henry H. Harrison's poetic prayer, I exclaim, "O Prince of Peace, make us content!"

"Very well," perhaps some expansionist may say, "but you should not pull down your barn before you can build a better one. What about the Philippines?" To this I would reply we can build a better one; and we are going to employ a master workman from the West to surperintend the work. It seems to me that no reasonable person would suppose that we should suddenly withdraw our army from the Philippines. But we can quit ourselves like men, high-minded men, and go to that Aguinaldo band of patriots, with honest confessions, and tell them, that, while a few of us, chiefly the McKinley Administration regime, had intended to compel you to become a colonial dependency of the United States, a majority of us after careful deliberating had decided that it was neither best for you nor for ourselves to do so. We are duty bound, though, to see that a government is adopted for you which shall secure life, liberty and the pursuit of happiness to all, and we mean that that government shall be entirely independent of the United States. Now, while we have had such regard for you as to deliver you from the bonds of colonizing conspiracies, and while we are yet obliged to see that you adopt a just government, equally administered, and modeled after that of the United States, a goverment of yourselves, for yourselves, and by yourselves, we shall ask that government to pay our future expenses incurred in the pursuance of this course, and when this government shall have been put in perfect working order, we shall leave you an independent nation. Will you consent to these propositions and lay down your arms?

Methinks, I hear the assenting voice of the Aguinaldo constituency thundering in grateful tones across the Pacific, that sea of peace which only divides us, over the mountain barriers to the uttermost parts of our country, and echo wafting back to the Philippines our right good will, instead of a deceitful lust for blood and gold. We should need to make such a treaty as I have suggested very specific, and the Philippinos will assent to it. If they should not, then we would be justified in shooting. But we shall not have to shoot. We shall need to restrict ourselves very conscientiously in the treaty, though, in order to gaurantee to the Philippinos that we are not trying to mislead them. The kind of government which we would put in operation, the maximum limit of expenses, and the length of time required to do the work should be stipulated in the treaty. This can all be done. I believe we would be justified in shooting if the Philippinos would not consent to such a treaty, because our position is such that we are morally bound to secure protection to the foreign residents of those islands, and the natives which want enduring peace and freedom. There is no reason why we cannot graft upon them a better government than Spain has imposed upon them, and there is is no reason why they cannot pay us for it out of their resources. We would be justified in adopting this course toward the Philippinos, and we would secure its justification at the hands of any rational tribunal, terrestrial or celestial, which we should desire always to do in all our actions as a Christian nation.

We would be justified in pursuing such a course and exacting from the Philippinos payment of our expenses in that course, for it is right, and it is the only way I see we can clear ourselves of iniquity in our relations with them. Such a course would deliver them from darkness and bondage into the light of liberty and civilization. But we would never be justified in asking them to pay our expenses, which we incurred in conducting this iniquitous war against them, up to the time we proposed to them their independence; for the dictators of the McKinley Administration have had wrong motives to lead them in their conduct of this war. Their motives have been to keep the Philippinos in bondage and subjection, and that, too, as a dependency of a civilized nation—a nation whose cherished declaration has always been that, just governments derive their powers from the consent of the governed; a nation which has always stood for freedom and the equality of all men before the law; a nation whose people with pride have always pointed their youth to the noble character of Wm. Penn, which is portrayed in his conversation with King Charles concerning the American Indians, and in the history of his dealings with them; a nation which, with great display of moral feeling, recently reached down to raise the Creoles of Cuba from bondage to freedom. Is such a nation as this now going to approve the course of the McKinley dictators and make the Philippinos its bondsmen? Shall we, as a father pitieth *not* his children, adopt a following of colonized dependencies, and, as a writer of the Baltimore American suggests, establish a colonial bureau in the war department, (yes, there is where it belongs,) under a less exciting name? Never! Waft it on the rolling tide! Never!

"May our prayer for others be
That every people shall be free."

Why should we free the Cuban from the tyranny of another nation and make the Philippino our bondman? Surely, such a course would more nearly satisfy bigotry and greed than manifest a benevolent spirit. Have we not been at as much expense in Cuba's behalf as we have in conducting the iniquitous war in the Philippines? Have we not in a righteous humor (?) promised the Cubans an independent government. Why should not the Philippinos have an independent government also? Why should we not just as gratuitously cancel our expense account made in our relations with the Philippinos as to cancel the one made in behalf of Cuba, especially since our misconduct and our attempt to oppress these poor people have made it so great as it is? Are not the Philippinos so capable of self government as are the Cubans?

Although Admiral Dewey nor any other American may not have promised the Philippinos their freedom, Aguinaldo reasoned well when, as the Philippine Commission states, he issued a proclamation inducing the Philippinos to expect to obtain their freedom through the good offices of the government of the United States. He thought he was just as capable of enjoying life, liberty and the pursuit of happiness as was the Cuban Creole. And why should he not? By this very act he exhibited prudence and capabilities for statesmanship. He knew we declared war against Spain for the freedom of the oppressed Cubans, who were similarly oppressed by Spain as was his kindred, only perhaps more severely for their greater resistance.

The Philippine Commission may well denounce the severe rigor and strict censorship of the Spanish rule in the islands; but it may not well remain tacitly indifferent as to the condition of the Americans there, and their censorship and conduct toward the natives. I fear that if it were all exposed the better element of our population would be heard to wail, "*Eli, Eli, lama Sabachthani,*" "My God, why hast thou forsaken me." Then, too, some of our "would be" Baal Priests, who have no higher estimate of religion than even the Pharisaic, than that it consists in posing well in a good name before the people, may well pray repentently, "God be merciful to me, a sinner."

People of different nations are not much unlike regarding their tendencies toward moral and immoral conduct, when the chief prevailing conditions are alike. When immoral conditions are rife, and even reigning, those who are not much morally inclined are going to drift with those conditions into immorarlity. And they will be none the less apt to do so where King Greed is on the throne than anywhere else. Immorality in its various phases is bound to be fostered by him. King Greed was chief of the Spanish rule in the Philippines, and under his tutilage do we see cruelty and immoralty in their varied forms looming up, and being protected by a censorship so strict as to practically prevent the whole civilized world from knowing anything about it, until that censorship gave way to American censorship; and then, of course, it was all disclosed and wafted to the uttermost parts of the earth. And it is only the old accusation of the "kettle calling the pot black," in pantomine upon the world's stage, and any person with a sound mind that looks upon it, if disposed to be impartial, will agree that this is the correct interpretation of it. Yes, King Greed was on the throne in the Philippines under Spanish censorship, and he is now on the throne there under American censorship, and will be so long as we continue to exploit our power there for the purpose of keeping the Philippinos in bondage and annexing their dominion to our government against their will. So long as he is on the throne there under the auspices of any nation, he is going to foster vice and immorality and screen it from the world by his censorship. Why is American censorship any better than Spanish censorship if it is instituted for the same low degraded design—the oppression and bondage of an already down-trodden people? Surely a difference in their conscientiousness is hard to see. So long as King Greed rules our army in the Philippines, we had rather accept than doubt the greater part of the reports concerning immoral practices of many of our soldiers there. The soldiers of King Greed are apt to become a little greedy. He sets the example for them and promises them protection if they follow it; for it is by extortion and excess that he expects to make his reign profitable. He must get his emissaries and soldiers to pattern after him if he would succeed.

Admitting, then, that under the circumstances the soldier is likely to have a desire to satisfy greed, we must acknowledge that above all things else to be watched, save the devil and a greedy nation, is the *man* of greed. He will do almost anything that is immoral to gratify greed—the idol of his heart. And by so doing he will become so indifferent to nobility of action and purpose as to tolerate other immoral conditions which may not even have the slightest tendency to satisfy his greed.

Having these precepts, then, we need not wonder what the future condition of affairs in the Philippines will be if we adopt a colonial policy and continue a system of ransacking and carpet-bagging there. We need not wonder at the reports we have already heard as to unscrupulous conditions that obtain there. We need not wonder when we are told that sickness and death prevails among our soldiers as a result of disease contracted by their association with the natives. And in the light of the foregoing premises we need not be amazed or astonished when we learn that a few days ago the Secretary of War manifested his support to indecent customs, when he chartered a vessel at the expense of the government to transport a cargo of women, which he pleased to call wives and sweethearts of the soldiers, from New York to the Philippines. Who ever heard of such an act in the history of civilized warfare?—Transporting a cargo of women and dumping them down in a soldier's camp, where we are told pestilences exist worse than are known to the direst places of prostitution and disgrace in this country! Ay, truly, we must admit that the American soldier, even, lacks sound wisdom and discretion when he announces such invitation, whether it be by reason of his own fond affection and amiable moral intentions, or as a base pretense. The soldier is said to be comparatively idle in the Philippines; and though the strictest military discipline prevails, which we have reason to doubt, whenever idleness is enlisted under the banner cf greed it is likely to beget vice. The eye of reason penetrates the veil of American censorship to portray the present conditions that prevail; and to interpret the future, so long as King Greed is on the throne and the mere lust for blood and gold sways a dominating influence. If the Philippine soldiers and their so-called wives and sweethearts expect to ever come home again, the sooner we call them from that errand of prodigality and greed the better will we protect our people from the visitations of iniquity.

Contrast the life of a soldier or an officer who is sent on a mission of prodigality, bondage and greed, with the life of one whose mission is to foster prosperity, morality, liberty and enlightenment. Which one is it that will most likely deal with the people to whom he is sent with a feeling of fond anxiety? And which one is it that will act with a spirit of indifference regarding their moral and material prosperity? Oh, had we not better, if only for the sake of the boys in blue, even, grant the Philippino independance and lend him a helping hand amid his cries of "Excelsior," and his struggles in trying to ascend the steeps of civilization?

I know that censorship may try to refute logical hypotheses, but it cannot do it. Dictative expansionists may say that we are painting the picture too dark. They may say that the object of a United States colonial sovereignty in the Philippines is not to gratify greed. They may say that the object of such sovereignty there is not to make that people our bondmen or an inferior national caste; but I tell you this is not so, and they do not speak the truth when they say it. If they do not make them our bondmen in any sense, or an inferior caste, which is bound to be treated with indifference by superiors as soon as the line is drawn, there is only one thing else which they can do with them, and that is to give that 10,000,000 Philippinos citizenship, which would be a far greater crime committed against our national self-preservation than to make them our *eternal* bondmen.

The average Philippino is far inferior to the average American citizen to-day, and that being the case, is it wise statesmanship to make him a citizen? Have we not about as much of the inferior element among us already as we can hope to even up morally, socially, physically, intellectually, and financially; which we must do would we attain to heights of civilization not yet reached. We are compelled to do this and to carry this element which we already have with us to a broader enlightenment, or we may well not attempt the journey as a republic; for the republic may undergo transition before the desired goal is reached and assume an imperial state of being and then *lag*. It is a historically illustrated and corroborated fact that when republics are found separating their people into castes they are retrograding and speedily drifting toward imperialism and aristocratic rule.

Yes, it is unwise for a republic, which is the best form of government for the common people, to do anything which may have a tendency to divide its people into castes. To the expansionists who would make the Philippino either our bondman or citizen, with a pretense of elevating him, I say, "Thou hypocrite, first cast out the beam that is in thine own eye, and then shalt thou see *clearly* to cast the mote out of thy brother's eye." If we would be living monuments to the honor of the republic we must stand solidly for the interests, the elevation, and the equality, as near as possible, of all the people, and especially the common people.

I say regarding our own present conditions ft would not be wise to make the Philippino a citizen, as he is an inferior human to us; and we *dare* not make him our bondman in any sense, by adopting a colonial policy, because of reesons already stated and others which I shall presently elicit. But we *do dare* to grant him liberty and provide for him and the foreigners there a just and independent government, and also compel him to submit to that proposition. And I think that Aguinaldo and his constituency are fair and wise enough to peaceably submit to that proposition. I believe that by adopting that course the Philippinos would become imbued with well-founded hopes. They would look forward with expectation and desire for the elevation of their race. They would, if they have common sense, which we know they have, consider our nation as their friend, and they would be found incessantly and in multifarious ways knocking at our doors for help and entreating us to turn on the *true search-light of civilization* in such a manner that we could not refuse without detriment to ourselves in a pecuniary senese, as well as in disobedience to the Divine injunction "Let your light so shine before men that others seeing your good works may glorify your father which is in heaven." Then would we, as Wm. J. Bryan said, be sending school-teachers to the Philippines instead of soldiers. In this course lies the true solution of the Philippine problem. Ay, methinks we would soon hear them seeking admission to our national union with right good will. The "little upstart" would now and then be found seeking protection from the blasts of the world, by trying to hide under the folds of Uncle Sam's coat; and in a sense of co-operation and benevolence, in other words in the exercise of that "social spirit of nations," he may in accord with all righteousness and self-preservation occasionally protect the little urchin, yet probably not every time could he do it without treading upon the rights of other national personages. In this direction even, he will need to exercise discretion. Well have sages said, "Wisdom is the principal thing; therefore get wisdom." Uncle Sam is a dummy, but he can get wise people to think for him yet.

But let me say that the climax of my thought here is—and I would to God that I might be able to paint it in great brilliancy on the skies clear around our celestial dome, so that as long as the earth revolves every American citizen could read it as a precept and a warning worthy to be followed in this "trying hour," and in all future circumstances involving the question of expansion—It is this: Uncle Sam should *never* take that little thing under his coat to protect it with a view to adopting it into his family as an heir to his domain; for if he does there will soon be a "fuss" in his family that will result in the bond of union being broken, the loss of family sympathy, and the creation of jealousies and enmities which will stand as enduring barriers to prevent the free exercise of that "righteous co-operation" and God-like "social spirit of nations."

I claim we can *never*, with national prudence, admit the Philippinos, though that people's strength and physical beauty may range anywhere from what it is to that of Sampson, and though their wisdom may range anywhere from what it is to that of Solomon. May God protect our nation from admitting the Philippinos even when their will accords with such a proposition. The distinguished Mr. John Sherman publicly announced just before the election this year that he is opposed to annexing the Philippines against their will. I now would know if he favors annexing them should their will accord with such action. Dare he say he does? Dare any statesman say he does? Show him to me! I say he lacks wisdom or he is prompted to do so by some unrighteous and unpatriotic lust. What statesman would dare admit 10,000,000 inferior people to citizenship in this country? The question reminds me of the advice which my mother has often given me about marrying, and it sounds too proverbial to even be original with her.

I have heard her say "Never marry until you can better yourself." And I have found that this precept requires careful interpretation. When could I better myself? was a great question. And it now looms up before Uncle Sam in regard to his espousal to Miss Philippine.

CHAPTER II.

I do not wish to be understood as being opposed to marriage. But I say, Uncle Sam, you'd better watch. You poor old widower. You've got a family which is about as much as you can take care of. You'd better stay at home and attend to your own business, and quit your courtin', if you are courtin', like an old fogy. (There he comes now. I wonder if he has heard me.)

Uncle Sam, you seem troubled about something, It cannot be you are in love? Here is a chair. Sit down. Perhaps a little rest may do you good, and, possibly I can say something to cheer you up and benefit you.

You look so much worried, my good old man. You have so much to attend to and so many family cares devolving upon you. And it seems like your cares are becoming more numerous and varied every day, too. Uncle Sam, do you think you could stand the pressure if your family was twice as large as it is? I know you have wonderful vigor, but I don't believe you could. You'd collapse.

Uncle Sam, is the rumor that you are espoused to Miss Philippine true? Or is it only a jest? You really do seem bothered, but you don't look like a man in love, it seems to me. I can't think you're so old as to be getting childish—Really are you in love with Miss Philippine?

If you are I don't want you to become insulted with me now, because I have always been devoted to you, and I am going to tell you for your own good, that if you are in love with Miss Philippine I don't think you ought to be. Because, Dear Uncle, I think you are getting too old to marry, and your circumstances won't justify it. Besides, if they would, I don't think that Miss Philippine is the girl for you. She is not adapted to you at all, and even if she were, don't you think she is too far away from home? I think if you would do a little courtin' you might find somebody nearer home that would suit you better—but, pshaw, Uncle, talk about you courtin' and marryin'! Nonsense! I don't think it would be for your good for you to do any courtin', or to get married, at all.

I have something in my little library which I read sometime ago that may help you to form a very wise decision. If you will tarry I will read it to you. Here is some of it. Tennyson says—Now, mind you, I do not mean to compare Miss Philippine to a savage, but I say, though, she deserves credit for what she is under the circumstances, she is inferior to you, and for that reason, among others, she is not adapted to you. I know you would not think of marrying a savage for her wealth if she were as rich as John Bright. But I think as Miss Philippine is your inferior, what Tennyson says here may be construed as having some bearing upon your case, if you are allured in any way by her sweet seducing charms. He says here:

"I, to herd with narrow foreheads, vacant of our glorious gains;
Like a beast with lower pleasures, like a beast withlower pains.

"Mated with a squalid savage, what to me were sun or clime;
I the heir of all the ages in the foremost files of time.

"I that rather held it better men should perish one by one,
Than that earth should stand at gaze, like Joshua's moon in Ajalon.

"Never, though my mortal summers to such 'length of years should come,
As the many wintered crow that leads the clanging rookery home."

And then this wise old bard says over here, in another place:

"The jingling of the guinea helps the hurt that honor feels,
And the nations do but murmur, snarling at each other's heels.

Uncle Sam, you'd better be careful. It seems to me I have heard you handling a good deal of money lately. Have you been taking it in or giving it out? Have you been fingering any English guineas? Do you think it is right to marry for money? Can it be that a man who is as well fixed as you are, and as wise as you are, would marry for money without any consideration for the things you marry with it? My mother has often said "Beware of marrying for money" and I think it is a good exhortation. Uncle Sam, cheer up now old man and own to the corn. Would you think of trying to love and marry Miss Philippine, your inferior, because *only think* she has money? What are you smiling about? Your own folly? Or at the thought of your relatives becoming so much agitated over a false rumor? Yes, I am certain, it is only the thought of the agitation of your people over this false rumor that causes you to smile. I know you are not such an old fogy as to think of trying to love and marry Miss Philippine under the circumstances, and even when she hasn't exhibited the slightest inclination to such thoughts toward you, but has been trying to buffet you ever since the rumor was started. I know you have more sense than to mistake her little proffered co-operation for her deliverance from bondage, for a fond love for you.

Longfellow says, "who can tell what thoughts and visions fill the fiery brains of young men?" But I cannot be mistaken as to the thoughts that play upon your braincells in regard to this affair. You know full well that your marriage to Miss Philippine, your inferior, would probably cause mental degeneration among the members of your family with whom she would associate, and you are too wise to err in this matter. You are right wary of a decline of intelligence.

You know, as Shakespeare says, "There was a time when it the brains were out the man would die." Why Uncle Sam you seem to smile an approval of what I have said. Here is your hat. Good morning, sir.

Well, the poor old man is gone. He seemed to enjoy my little talk. He is a good old man, and I believe he thinks a good deal of me. I should certainly be very sorry to see him get into trouble about anything, much less a silly courtship, which a man in his circumstances shouldn't think about.

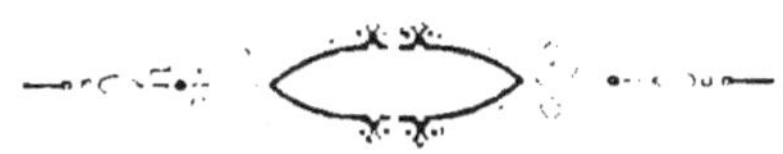

CHAPTER III.

I can not believe there is a statesman in the land, even a follower of President McKinley, or he himself, who would think of making the Philippino a citizen, and granting him representation in our legislative halls, to-day. This being the case, let us now see what course would most probably be followed should we not place him on a footing of independence. There is only one other course to be taken and that is to adopt an iniquitous colonial policy; and all will admit that the only advantage which can be gained thereby is a pecuniary one, and that the extent of that pecuniary advantage is embraced in the extent of the assets of our *oppression* and *taxation* in one form or another above the liabilities incurred by our various mutinous institutions. Oppression and taxation without representation, which Patrick Henry in the climax of all his sublime patriotic eloquence called *tyranny*, and taxation which President McKinley in a modern political campaign tirade would deceitfully or through ignorance make the people believe is *not* tyranny. Well did Wm. J. Bryan say, "If we adopt a colonial policy; if we pursue a course which excited the Revolution of 1776, we must muffle the tones of Old Liberty Bell, and speak in dusky whispers when we praise the patriotism of our forefathers." His words are like apples of gold in pictures of silver. Expansionists are not saying much about the nature of the proclamation of Old Liberty Bell and our forefathers just now; and when they do they always evade the applicable truth, or put a perverse construction upon it; something like, "Taxation without representation is *not* tyranny."

If we adopt a colonial policy in the Philippines the only purpose in it is to extort them of their wealth and thus institute a system of drainage upon the essentials of their vitality and subsistence. Now can we by these exactions and extortions better prepare them by force for citizenship? I say no! no! And we should thank Providence that we can not; for it is not best for us to have their citizenship. This being the case, then the question naturally arises: Shall we act toward them with intentions of making them citizens at some future date, when in all probability they will not be as well qualified for citizenship as they now are, or shall we act toward them with a view to making them our perpetual bondmen? God forbid that we should do either. It would be imposing injustice as great as the unjust taxation itself. And we would at sometime bring in the harvest of all this evil sowing; for truly, "Whatsoever a man soweth that shall he also reap." All history, in every instance, proclaims to us that bitter fruits have always been brought home by every people who have attempted to enslave another in any way. And all history argues and decides that we cannot, by imposing a colonial policy of extortion and excess upon the Philippino, better prepare him for citizenship.

We should remember that even the colonizing systems of European monarchies are far superior, and that most of them are far more humane and fostering in their nature than any we could possibly devise for the Philippines. We should remember that it has been a vital principle in nearly all their colonizing plans to send settlers from among their own people and their own race, whom they had a paternal fondness for, and whom, in most instances have gone to subdue savage wilds, and develop sparsely settled districts. Dare we attempt to bring such purposes of colonization down to a level with any policy we could devise for the Philippines? Contrast such systems with our purposes, to go out among our antipodes, to a territory more thickly settled than our Southern States would be, were the whole population of the Union crowded into them—to a territory with 10,000,000 people thus thickly settled, and of another race, whom we, as well behaved human beings, have no paternal fondness or natural affection for, save a brotherly love, which would begin to steadily decline as soon as the domineering process was instituted. The fraternal love of any two brothers, one of whom is thought by both to be accorded more liberty than the other, is going to wane and even degenerate into jealosy which will cause trouble. Contrast the European systems of colonization instituted for the purpose of finding homes for their dense populations in sparsely settled districts, among savage wilds, with our system proposed for the Philippines, which is instituted for nothing in God's world but to gratify greed; and then dare say, in the broad light of reason, that should we adopt this system we should ever criticise monarchical institutions.

Think what a fallacy it is for a nation that has undeveloped resources within its domain to provide for the natural increase of population for the next 150 years to go to the opposite side of the globe and institute a cruel system of "taxation without representation" upon an already over-populated territory. Is it not the greatest manifestation of greed, hoggishness and nonsense every heard of? Shame come upon the American voter who would support such a proposition! Oh! I say, be wary, or the unrighteous exercise of your ballot may prove to be "the mark of the beast in the forehead or in the hand." Shall this government which has denounced taxation without representation as tyranny, and which has always opposed the advance of monarchical institutions, now institute a colonial policy which monarchies might well consider beneath their dignity? If it should, it would by so doing nicely pantomime the life and fate of Capt. Wm. Kidd, who went out to capture sea pirates and in so doing became the greatest of them all.

CHAPTER IV.

It is ridiculous and traitorous to talk of colonizing the Philippines with a view to preparing them for citizenship. And if we could do it, and should admit them to representative citizenship, I know of no other act that would better demonstrate to the world that our people were rapidly becoming incapacitated for self-government. Why, monarchies would cite such an act with sneers whenever popular government should be mentioned. It is with wise policy that European nations waive representative citizenship to colonies composed of their own kindred and posterity. England is well aware that for her to grant her colonies representation, to-day, would work her ruin. She was well aware that in the Colonial Period of this country it was not conducive to her best interests to even grant her beloved American colonies representation in Parliament—colonies composed of her own posterity and her own race; and rather than do so she would suffer them to declare independance in 1776, and meet them on the field of battle even, on that footing, give up her sovereignty, and suffer the gloom of defeat. And by so doing she set an example which republics, even, may do well to follow, especially when disgraced with a colonizing system imposed upon an alien race, She has studied Roman history too well to not know when that empire reached the zenith of her glory. She has studied ancient history too well to not know what caused the decline of all the world-wide empires. And she is now prospering and rearing her name above other nations of the earth, by the counter-example set by the nations before her.

It is exceeding puerile for our people to think of expanding our territorial limits, much less opening the doors of our legislative halls to the various alien peoples thereby encompassed. No; It would be unwise to make the Philippino a citizen; it would be unwise to make him our eternal bondman; but it would be wise and righteous to treat with him on a footing of independence and to compel him to submit to it should he refuse to do so.

There is only a mere doubtful pecuniary advantage to be gained by not granting him independence, and to maintain that we would impede his advancement in civilization, and imperil our own beloved country with a colonial policy--a great sneaking, lurking, chronic disorder--an expansion malady, which would certainly at some day work disaster and ruin to our nation, the grand memento and handiwork which we have inherited by virtue of the wisdom of our forefathers.

Capitalists can be honorable; and doubtless many are. (But I would make millionaires who have safe investments ashamed to farther accumulate or to live in prodigality amid the hungering and distress, the sorrow and heartache in our land, when they could so grandly utilize their surplus income.)

I fear there are capitalists promulgating expansion for the

love of money, which, by hardening their hearts they have mistaken for patriotism. A strong appeal to their consciences, which they have greatly smothered with evil desires, might incline them to follow not the forbidden path. I fear there are capitalists who for the sake of greed would favor expansion or any other evil. I fear there are capitalists who for the sake of greed would convert our republic into an empire which would pay them tribute. I fear there are capitalists who would supersede the natural competency and independence of the laboring class with artificial incompetency and dependence upon a vain, besotted, gourmandized aristocracy. I fear there are capitalists who have already conceived the immigration of the pauper class of Philipinos. I fear there are capitalists who too much desire mutual combination of capital and diversity and opposition of labor. I fear there are capitalists who know that if we adopt the Philippino he could come to this country as a citizen in spite of any consistent legislation, and should he come, they could send him to the polls with his ballot as a tribute to their greedy desires.

I hope I am mistaken in these presumptions. I wish I were. But observation and consciousnessness would make me believe I am not.

To the gross immoral sensualist who views nothing in national affairs as patriotic except that which in some way pays homage to greed, let me say again, and with all the emphasis I can summon, that the advantage to be gained from adopting the Philippino is even pecuniarily a most doubtful one.

If we should strive against the decrees of Almighty God so plainly exemplified in history; If we should undertake the blasphemy of brandishing the sword over an unwilling people to make them christians; If we should forcibly impose taxation upon the Philippines; If we should undertake the absurdity of forcibly enthroning commerce, which always rests upon amity; If we should do all this, then, in order to perpetuate all this crime, a conservative estimate of the expenses of the requisite military regime is $60,000,000 per annum.

You will agree then that this amount must be overbalanced by the credits of oppression and taxation in order to make our licensed crime profitable in a pecuniary sense. Now, how under heaven are we to make $60,000,000 out of the Philippine establishment, when Spain, with the most odious and oppressive taxation, including a per capita tax on Chinese

Coolies, has only been able to realize about $13,500,000 a year from those islands? Is it possible we shall plunder those innocent people worse than Spain? Any sensible person should know, that owing to new conditions that would prevail, we should have to plunder that people much worse than Spain of we would even realize the meager sum of $13,500,000, as she did. The United States would undoubtedly want free trade for herself in the Philippines and the extent of her trade there would detract just that much from her revenues.

Considering this matter in all the light of understanding, we must conclude, that by this course of force and might against right, there is to be gained not even a pecuniary advantage, but on the other hand a deficit of something like $50,000,000 will be exhibited annually, which must be raised by taxation at home or leave our nation in debt. Why, it seems to me that an expansionist is not capable of reasoning on financial matters.

Dare he say this deficit will be made up in increased trade? Dare he say we can afford to create this national deficit, because it will be many times repaid in trade? Then I answer, first, that a true republic would know no castes among its people, and will not thus legislate to benefit certain classes and oppress the masses. Then I would say, secondly, that *we can not make up this deficit by increased trade secured by such a course.* The relative locations of the United States and the Philippines, and the climatic and geographical differences won't admit of our so doing. I would say, as Andrew C. Carnegie has said—Andrew C. Carnegie, the ablest and best financial friend President McKinley ever had in all his sixteen years in Congress, and the one who always contributed largely to the campaign fund that helped to keep him there—Andrew C. Carnegie said, "The Manufacturer of England, Germany or France, the farmer of Australia, the Baltic Provinces of Russia and the Agentine reach the Philippines at about one-half the freight cost that the American farmer has to pay upon his products or the American Manufacturer has to pay upon manufactured articles."

I would say also that if we discriminated by granting ourselves free trade in the Philippines, and imposing against other countries the most consistent tariff for revenue, the balance of trade would then be against us and in their favor; for their freight charges and revenue duties included would not amount to the freight charges alone in our trade.

Trade drifts in natural channels, and all man can do is to play upon its current. He can not make the current run up hill by any force he would uselessly summon, were it intended to run down hill. And every time he undertakes to modify it in the least, he is going to do just that much work in the world for nothing; and his outlay in every instance will be equal to his income, and in the major offenses will far surpass his income; and after all his efforts, his little artificial stream of trade is going to trickle back into the great natural one, in obedience to fate and Divine Wisdom.

Tell me that we have any business in the Philippines! Why you might as well undertake to make me believe that a West Virginia farmer should always have a potato patch in California!

May God help us to be careful.

Truly, "Eternal vigilance is the price of virtue."

CHAPTER V.

Well, if we can not, with impunity to ourselves and the Philippines, enforce our power there; let us turn the tables once more upon the footing of independence.

If we should propose to form for the Philippinos an independent government, and put it into good working order, which we are now morally bound to do; if we should promise to assign to him at some future date, (the date should be specified,) entire control of that government, provided he agree to pay our stipulated expenses in organizing it for him, and protecting it in its incipiency; methinks the result would be that the animosity of the Philippino would gradually melt before our true searchlight of civilization like an April snow before the sun. He would take courage. He would view the future with bright prospects. He would, and well may he, gladly pay e reasonable redemption fee for his deliverance from the bonds of Spanish cruelty and the American Expansionists' schemes of extortion. He would doff his military garb, and convert the battle field into a grain field. He would, with prospects of a bright future, incline his attention toward those pursuits which would provide food for his hungry, education for his ignorant, morality and religion for his immoral and treacherous, and perpetual liberty and self-government for his now down-trodden and oppressed people. Philippino opposition now extant would then be converted into Philippino assistance in our work for his sake. And our $60,000,000 expenses annually there, would be minimized to less than $13,500,000, the amount of revenues now collected, and the $13,500,000 revenue, owing to increase of trade and the application of the energy of the Philippino now engaged in war to the various oivil pursuits in life and liberty, would be augumented to beyond $60,000,000. Such a condition would imbue the Philippino with a hope of soon paying us for the exercise of our good offices for his redemption, and such a condition would happily inspire our people at home and our soldiers and officers engaged to do the good work in the Philippines with a heartier moral courage.

We should make it a point in the period of governimental organization in the Philippines to be very careful to appoint the Philippino to office whenever his capabilities will admit of our so doing. We should institute and organize original states in such sections as are most favorable, and form for these original states a union, and provide for elections and statute laws which may be adapted to the requirements. We should provide also for the admission of new states that may afterward be formed. We should place his government on a firm bais for his benefit and not ours. In doing all this we should keep self in the background, realizing that at the end of the specified period we were going to "stir the nest" and let the little eaglet look out for itself. The true laborer is only worthy of his hire, and that is all he expects.

That the average Philippino is a being inferior to the average American citizen, I do not doubt. But they deserve credit for what they are at the hands of extortion. Many of them are well qualified for usefulness in the various vocations.

Say they are not capable of intellectual improvement, or say they are uneducated as a whole, and you say a lie. Many of them are peers to our average American college graduates. Many Philippinos have been educated in Europe. I often hear our college graduates say that they would like to take a course in a European college. Why, the Philippine Congress contains eighty-four members who are graduates of European colleges, and yet greed has branded them as ignorant outlaws. It is an injustice to the cause of righteousness and a shame upon our nation, that we do not grant this people freedom, and let the better element of it go to work with a fostering love and a fond anxiety for the elevation and advancement of its own race.

The Philippine Commission could not more conclusively exhibit its partiality and reverence for King Greed than it does by citing a whole prologue in its report to bring out the false inference, that it thinks that inasmuch as the Philippinos have only been fighting for a redress of grievances for the last three hundred years and not for independance, they should not now fight for independence, and should not have it.

Should our forefathers, who conceived our independence for us while we were yet fighting for a redress of grievances, rise from their graves, and in a review of the fullness of their honor pass by this Philippine Commission, its members could only, with deference to themselves, hang their heads in shame until the procession had passed.

The Philippine Commission should remember that we were fighting in one way or another, with tongue or pen or sword, through centuries also for a redress of grievances only, and that the Revolutionary War was in the beginning a fight for a redress of grievances. Will they say that that was any reason why we should not have indepedence? Would they have stepped up to Thomas Jefferson while he was writing that glorious declaration of rights, and have told him that the American Colonies did not now deserve liberty because they had only been fighting for a redress of grievances? Then right bitterly methinks he would have rebuked them. Why, we should better tear down the turf that wraps the clay of our forefathers, and have dragged the Statue of Washington in its entirety from our Capitol steps amid the Dewey celebrities, than to thus dishonor the spirit of our martyred patriots.

"Whatsoever ye would that men should do unto you, do ye even so to them."

CHAPTER VI.

A great humanitarian and theologian has said, "For $20,000,000 we have purchased of Spain a tablet upon which to write the epitaph of the nation." Now, although there is truthful significance in his words, it seems to me we are a right "lively corpse" yet. And if we have purchased the tablet for God's sake let us not recognize a decline by writing our own epitaph. We can use that tablet for better purposes. It was a mistake to have bought it unless it was our intention to shape it into a statue which would symbolize freedom and denounce tyrany throughout the world. We can use it in this way yet. Will we do it?

Some may say we can't afford to use the tablet for this purpose and lose the 20,000,000. I would say we had far better use it for the statue than to let it lie idle; because we don't want to set it up as our own tombstone. We have paid the $20,000,000, instead of which all we can claim is the tablet. I fancy making the double faced statue of it rather than a tombstone; even if by making it a tombstone we should regain the $20,000,000 and have the tombstone also. I dare you to measure life, patriotism and justice by the almighty dollar. We should better throw the $20,000,000 to the dogs than to have need to order for ourselves a tombstone by trying to regain that $20,000,000,—and with usury, as Senator M. A. Hanna might suggest.—Why, our revenues now amount to something like $2,000,000 a day, and we are now prodigalty spending millions every month. And it doesn't seem to hurt us, so President McKinley said. Is such a nation as this going to barter its existance? or, like Esaw, sell its birthright for a mess of pottage? or write its own epitaph and pose under it in the arms of death throughout the ages that shall roll? And all to regain, by extorsion, the paltry sum of $20,000,000, which was mistakenly applied or which was paid for the material out of which to build the double-faced statue? Shall President McKinley in the midst of his glorious successes for the redemption of the Cubans wisely erect from the Philippine Tablet that double-faced statue? I can not help believing that he bought it for the statue. But I fear that by the tumult of his Spanish War record and the vanity of his advisors he has been led into forbidden paths. I fear that he is chiseling the tablet for the nation's tombstone, and carving the first letters of the inscription. Oh, may he retrace his steps and remodel his work, or will some one else take it up?

I think that of the two wrongs we would far better lose the $20,000,000 than to colonize the Philippines. But we shall not need to do either. The Philippines will righteously pay this as a part of their redemption; but they will not pay any other expenses which we may have incurred in our relations with them up to the date of treating with them on a basis of independence. It may be well to claim in part payment of this $20,000,000, an island or a port or two, which we may need as a coaling and naval station. All we need, and all we should have for our own good, outside of our Continuous Domain and Alaska, is a few naval stations here and there, wherever new avenues of trade are naturally opened up. We should no. want Hawaii, nor Cuba, nor the Philippines, nor even Porto Rico. I am opposed to continued expansion, and I believe it means retrogression and trouble.

CHAPTER VII.

I am twenty-seven years of age to-day, and of that twenty-seven years I have been in the school-room twenty-one years, the last ten of which I have been engaged in teaching. I have gradually imbibed a fond patriotism and an unselfish anxiety for the future welfare of our people, and the boys and giris who have been under my tutilage, and those like them throughout our land. I think that my study of geography and his.ory and my efforts in my teaching for others' sake has chiefiy done this good work for me. I remember some things incidental to the involution of my mental attainments, whatever they may be. I remember how my early knowledge of geography revolved itself in my mind.

I was direc.ed to the map of our Contiguous Domain, and was told that it was our country, and that happily, it was one of the grandest on the globe. Then it was explained to me why it was so great and grand, and naturally I began to love it; because of its location, its resources, the li tle scattering facts of history I had picked up—like the "hatchet story"—all this and because it was our country I loved it.

The while before I knew about Alaska, whenever my eye caught sight of our map, and very often in my imaginations of it, there would flash throughout my being a pleasant and almost indescribable feeling—satisfaction, comfort, consolation, competency and gratitude are words which may help to describe it. I thought our country was the grandest country on the globe, and had the prettiest map in the geography. I admired its shape, even the Peninsula of Florida and the little buttress at Minnesota. It was so neatly bounded on the north by Conada, on the east by the Atlantic, on the south by Mexico and the Gulf, and on the west by the Pacific. Oh, I did love it!

Then one day I was told that Alaska was a part of the United States. It was hard for me to believe it. I know just how I felt. I wished it wasn't so. But later I was told that it was very valuable for its furs and fisheries, and its lumber and minerals, and it was yet thinley settled, and owing to climate it would never contain a vary dense population; and that for all these reasons we did well to get it.—Well, I submitted. I had to adapt my mind to the decree. I tried to associate Alaska with the United States as well as I could; and I did it without much effort, too. Whenever my mind imaged the map of the United States, there was Alaska—there it hung away out there by itself with the southern extension as a handle pointing this way, as if saying, "hold me." But I gradually gained patience and resignation, and even thought it was better to have Alaska; and that it would do very well for a back-yard if we did have to go to it in a boat.

But, oh, how dark and gloomy were my forebodings when I learned that w ewere about to secure Hawaii? By this time I had gained some knowledge of general history. I knew that it was expansion that proved fatal to the great empires before us, and that without the instrumentality and forethought of wise statesmanship, insatiate greed would, in this way, get the best of us, too. My prayer was that we would not meddle with Hawaii. And I made a solemn vow, as did Lincoln when he saw the slaves sold at the block and driven off like cattle, that if I could ever use my influence to check this crime against the nation which our forefathers conceived in blood and tears for us, I would do it.

CHAPTER VIII.

It seems to me that our Republican friends are going to get their tariff and expansion ideas muddled. The two are incompatible unless they eke in, in some way, the word "bondage" or "sectional discrimination." If they have free-trade with Hawaii, Cuba, Porte Rico, and the Philippines, as we have between our states, that will be just that much free-trade, won't it? At least that is the way I view it. If they should have the whole world under Uncle Sam's coat I wonder which they would have, free-trade or sectional discrimmation. I expect they would choose the latter; and they would have a great muss of it, too, in a short while.

From this line of thought, as also many others, any reasonable man will conclude that we should appose expansien if we would avoid trouble, preserve *this nation* intact, and stand for the peace of the world. If a nation absorbs others about it, it will lose its identity, and this will cause patriotism to wane and sectional jealousy to arise.

It fills my heart with grief to think that our expansionist friends are so unwise as to argue, that because we have profited by expansion in the past we will continue always to profit by it; that because Thomas Jefferson bought the territory of Louisiana we should hold fast to the Philippines; that because our forefathers acted wisely by expnnding our territorial limits, it would be wise to continue expansion. Crabapples could not agonize my feelings more than such argument.

I would that all men should agree that it is foolish and inexpedient for one nation to even attempt to legislate for the whole earth. I would that all men should agree that it was wise and expedient for our forefathers to expand the limits of our Contiguous Domain; and that there must, therefore, be a consistent mean to our territorial limits. Then I would that the American voters should agree, and forever so decide with their ballots, that the consistent mean of the territorial limits over which our grand government should be exercised is embraced in our Contiguous Domain and Alaska.

Then I would that our government should be so nearly righteous that other governments might typify with profit. But let us discontinue the greedy absorption process, and establish our national identity of continued being. Then with a normal stature, mature and in good health, let us go about our life-work, throughout which we shall let our light so shine before men that others, seeing our good works, may thereby glorify our Father which is in heaven. This is the *true spirit of patriotism*, and in it can we turn upon the world the *true search-light of civilization*, which will shine so bright as to cause the demons of sin to seek their more secluded allotment.

The immature corn is unfit for use, and the ear that expands until it bursts the shuck, rots. Methinks, this is the text from which our expansionist forefathers would now preach to our greedy friends.

Expansionists should remember that our past territorial expansion is quite different from the proposed colonial policy.

Whenever territories have been acquired in the past they have been immediately placed upon a basis of freedom and self-government. Their people have been as surely guaranteed protection of life, liberty and the pursuit of happiness as have the people of any other state in our Union. So sure and well known is this guarantee to the territories that our citizens migrate from the states to them without the least doubt that they may thereby lose any of their liberties as citizens. Discrimination between any other state or section in our Union and these territories is strictly and plainly forbidden by our Federal Law. And our laws also guarantee to these territories legislative powers in our government as soon as they are found to contain the required population. There can be no inequalities in Federal Taxation throughout the United States and the organized territories thereof. So reads the law.

Would our expansionist friends have any inequalities between the Philippines and our States? If so, they are, through the instrumentality of King Greed, instituting bondage and creating castes in our republic, which is *treason*. If they would not have discriminating taxation in the Philippines, or there execute predatory schemes of some kind, then, in the name of God and for the sake of humanity, I would ask: What are we fighting for? I would ask: What advantage it would be to us to hoist our flag by force over the Philippino, give him a seat in congress and grant the Malay race legislative powers in our government. We already have two races there represented, and many consider that a fact grievous to be borne. But we cannot, with justice, refuse to carry that fact since the two races are found under our flag. We can only profit by looking with compassion upon our weaker and down-trodden brother in either race, and by trying to elevate him. And this is quite enough for us to do at present. We should have no desire to place the Malay race under our flag, or to cause it to immigrate upon our people.

Why not redeem the Philippino and equip him for competency and independance, at a reasonable fee? Think of it—to enforce our power over the Philippino for the purpose of extorsion, or to make him a citizen. It makes my heart sick. Well may the preacher say it is vanity.

CHAPTER IX.

"What is a man profited if he gain the whole world and lose his own soul?"—Matt. 16–26.

What is a nation profited if it gain the whole world and then lose all, even that which it now hath? What shall it profit the United States to continue expansion and get into trouble, which we would do if we should make our new possessions bond or free? If we will have a colonial policy of discrimination, then the American Geslers shall meet their oppressed on the field of battle, for so always to tyrants it shall be—"*Sic Semper Tyrannis.*" Or if instead of colonial discrimination we should choose diversities of representative citizenship, diversities of races under our flag, diversities of geographical and commercial conditions, then we shall also have diversities of civil strife. For so long as we have a variable climate in the world which nurtures variety in races, variety in human temperament, variety in occupations, variety in manners and customs of people; and so long as man shall be easily led into sin by showing partiality and exhibiting his selfishness; so long it was intended that one nation should not rule the earth or any greatly diversified part of it. History has illustrated this. Every nation that has adopted the continued expansion policy has been found to practice unjust discrimination, which, sooner or later, proved to be ruinous and fatal.

If this policy were not practiced we would not notice the ushering in of new nations upon the world's history so frequently, and the ushering out of the old. We would not notice such irregularities and complexities in the boundaries and make-up of the countries of the old world to-day. The mountain barriers of History and Geography, which lie across every school-boy's line of march to the Valley of Educational Attainments, would not be so high and many of weaker courage would emigrate from the Plains of Ignorance, which are so noted for the production of that raw material called Misapplied Brains, out of which Vice is manufactured and shipped throughout the world. Oh, may wise policies be adopted for the countries of the New World, so that their boundaries may be established and always be pleasing to the eye, and their history a delight to study.

This infernal practice of governmental expansion and artificial control and modification of trade causes more sin and misery and heartache than all things else combined. It is Chief of the Devil's Staff in the world. It is the Demon that has, in all ages and in all climes, dared to venture out in the brilliant vitalizing sunlight and pure air, among our agricultural classes, and rob them of their vitality and happiness and leave them in poverty, distress and disease. It is the Demon that has congested the populations in great cities and driven the people to abodes amid the stench of foul alleys and the gases and smokes above the tenth story. It is the Demon which has done all this, and then stands "laughing in his sleeve" at the modern scientist trying to determine the cause of the advance of poverty, mortality, disease and crime.

If this Demon were driven from the face of the earth, then every human being would get a much better allotment of pure air, sunlight, wholesome food and all the bounties of art and nature. Then would poverty and gourmandized aristocracy, disease and mortality and crime, gradually vanish from among us, and human life would roll on to good old ages of modern Methusellahs.

Imagine, too, the enormous freight charge of useless shipping to these congested centers of manufacture and trade. It may do for the balance of the world to go to the Torrid Zone to trade for oranges, but it would be unwise and inexpedient to carry all structural material there, because oranges grow there, and have it there manufactured, and bring back the finished product.

Could not more of our manufacturers profit by coming out of the congested populations, noise and foul air of the city to the country town nearer their raw material? Would it not be better to let the common carriers do more useful carrying and less useless carrying? Would it not be better to let them carry more of the finiohed product and not so much raw material?

Common carriers are errand runners for the people and they deserve to be well paid for their work. But I tell you fellow laborers, farmers. and brother teachers, that it is a sign of a process of sap-sucking and abnormal conditions to see the managers and employees of carrier companies so much more prosperous than other classes.—Did I say employees? Yes, but I mean a *false prosperity* for *them*, at their expense as well as at the expense of other laborers. I mean that the total amount of money paid out to employees of common carriers is too much. Understand I don't mean that each employee is paid too much. I mean a majority of them are not paid enough. The money is not rightly distributed. There are too many of the boys "running extra" as they call it, making a few days in a month, enough to pay their board bill sometimes, and lying idle the balance of the time. It seems to me it would be better for them to work regular or quit and get at something else, and let the fellow that is retained work more regular. It is a shame to see how the human race is being whipped around and deluded and misled by the money power. Would it not be better if less money were paid to the employees and it were better distributed, and they had regular work at the same wages, or as nearly as possible, as they are now getting? Is it not a dangerous sign to see so many laborers begging their bread, you might say, from the common carriers, instead of earning a good living in their employment? And is it not more dangerous to see that they really *do* get this bread pieced out to them along the route by the carriers, when that bread does not belong to the carrier companies but to the people who started them on their errand? If these people should need to beg (which they do not naturally) why not let them beg that bread from the people who have earned it by their labor, and to whom it rightly belongs, instead of from these prodigal errand runners? And should we think, either, that this bread which is dished out to honorable paupers by these errand runners is nearly all that disappears? I think it is not. Have I herein encompassed a thought that manufacturers, farmers, laborers, professionalists and voters, would do well to consider? If I have, I hope they may do so, and when there is the least doubt leave it, also, in favor of the prisoner at the bar—the health of the human race.

What a horrible spectacle it is for a nation to practice expansive adhesion and assimilation, corrupting and decomposing its being by sapping the life-blood from the surface capillaries to congested centers within until the skin is sallow and the heart is sick. Truly, nations as well as individuals should have a normal size and a social spirit. Hawaii, or Cuba, or Porto Rico, or the Philippines can only be cancerous modifications of the normal structure of our nation.

I hope I shall not be accused of harboring any sectional prejudice against any part of our common country, for that does not rankle in my breast. I love our national heritage, and desire to see it only symmetrically developed in its entirety, to every nook and corner of its boundary. I would only see it undergo normal metamorphoses, passing on from its present marvelous attainments to more sublime and greater usefulness in the world. I would have its every act and volition conducive to the establishment of a character which might be approved by Omnipotent Justice as a model for the world. And I believe that our national heritage, through a righteous guidance of the people would attain to a glory which would excite the admiration of the most sanguine. This country is so located, geographically and commercially, and endowed with such vast resources, as to make it, if it considers and acts toward others with good will and charity, the most glorious nation the world shall ever have known. Of course it would be impracticable, but if it were necessary, it could better exist independent of trade and communication with the outside world than any nation on the globe.

I would see this nation attend to its own business and utilize every part of its own estate, and not encroach upon its neighbors' farms, since a farmer can be a benefit to his neighbor without tresspassing. I believe, since it is happily a fact that the North and the South and the West are within our domain, that it is more conducive to the symmetrical development and utilization of the entire country to have, proportionately, more manufacturing done at the North, more cotton raised at the South, and more wheat raised in the West. But it does not follow that either section cannot be utilized in many other ways, or that there is any need of congesting populations in manufacturing and commercial centers.

I think that if the people of our country consider their own interest as a nation, they will realize, also, that the nation can do more good for the people of the outside world, by neither espousing their governments, nor coveting their inheritance, nor encroaching upon their territory. I believe it is our duty, as a nation of power, influence and character, to assist our down-trodden brother throughout the world in every way we can, even though sometimes at our own expense; but by so doing it is neither necessary nor expedient for us to become espoused to them or covet their possessions.

" Do you slumber in your tent Christian Soldier,
While the foe is spreading woe though the land ?
Do you note his rising power growing bolder every hour ?
Will he not our land devour while you stand."

"Let us arise, all unite,
Let us arise in our might,
Let us arise speak for God and the right."

CHAPTER X.

In order to protect themselves and other American states from the selfishness and greed of European nations, our people have adopted the precious Monroe Doctrine, which implies that any attempt by a European nation to gain dominion in America shall be considered by the United States as an unfriendly act.

I would suggest that in connection with this cherished Monroe Doctrine, and in order to protect themselves and others from the selfishness and greed of our own nation, that the people adopt the doctrine that any attempt by the rulers of this nation to extend our sovereignty beyond Alaska and our Contiguous Domain shall be considered as an unfriendly act.

I would regard the establishment of this doctrine more important to our national self-preservation than the establishment of the Monroe Doctrine. Yet, both are wholesome and beautiful, and deserve to be cherished by our people, and handed down to the hearts of succeeding generations by history and tradition.

Show me a true Christian gentleman, and I will show you a man who considers it more important to guard against his own selfishness than the selfishness of others. Show me a good and truly enlightened nation, and I will show you a nation which considers it more important to guard against its own selfishness than the selfishness of other nations. We, as a nation, or as individuals, need to watch both our own selfishness and the selfishness of others.

Trusting that God may help our people to see the importance of this doctrine, I now submit this manuscript, as a work of supplication and thanks on this Thanksgiving Day, 1899, with the poetic benediction of Henry H. Harrison:

No Empire—Save it be Thine Own!

God of our Fathers whose command
Parted the waters from the land,
And led our grandsires here—that we
Might dwell in peace and liberty,
Be with us in this trying hour,
And save us from the Tempter's power!

Ruler of Battles! who sustained
The patriot armies' till they gained
Our freedom from the kings of earth,
Who gave the great republic birth,
Grant that the nation still may see
The star of hope, of liberty!

Grant that this people still may lead
The onward march Thou hast decreed,
And may our glorious mission be—
To lead mankind to liberty—
Until the time appointed brings
The coming of the King of Kings!

Son of the Morning! who hast known
How to refuse an earthly throne,
Grant us, too, that grace to make that choice
And heed not Satan's tempting voice,
Or money-changers, who would sell
And league us to the powers of hell!

Grant that this land may know no throne,
No empire—save it be Thine Own,
No empire built with fire and sword,
No empire stained with tears and blood,
No empire o'er unwilling slaves,
O'er ashes, bones and patriot graves!

Grant that the great republic's name
May never bear the robber's shame,
Nor Yankee lust for blood and gold
Call down the doom of empires old!
Grant that the needless blood we shed
Be not upon our children's head!

O Prince of Peace! make us content
With our own boundless continent,
Not sending armies o'er the waves
To make far distant nations slaves;
And may our prayer for others be—
That every people may be free!

Rebuke the hypocrites who claim
To conquer others in Thy name,
The blasphemy which would compel
Thy Gospel spread with shot and shell,
The Baal priests who stay to teach
And fill their pockets while they preach!

Lord God of Sabbaoth! when we fight,
May it be only for the right,
And not to plunder those who stand
For freedom and their native land!
From blood and spoil make us forbear!
God of the Patriot! hear our prayer!

www.ingramcontent.com/pod-product-compliance
Lightning Source LLC
Chambersburg PA
CBHW021600270326
41931CB00009B/1313

9783337007812